KEANU REEVES

A Legacy in Action – From the Matrix to John Wick

Herbert K. Howard

Copyright @ 2024 By Herbert K. Howard

All rights reserved. No part of this book may be reproduced, distributed, or transmitted in any form or by any means, including photocopying, recording, or other electronic or mechanical methods, without the prior written permission of the publisher, except in the case of brief quotations embodied in critical reviews and specific other noncommercial uses permitted by copyright law.

Content

INTRODUCTION
  The Enigma of Keanu Reeves
CHAPTER 1: EARLY BEGINNINGS
  From Beirut to Toronto: Keanu's Roots
  Discovering a Passion for Performance
CHAPTER 2: BREAKING THROUGH – THE ROAD TO FAME
  The Rise of Ted: A Comedic Icon
  Speeding to Stardom: "Speed" and the Action Star
CHAPTER 3: THE MATRIX EFFECT
  Becoming Neo: The Role of a Lifetime
  The Cultural Impact of "The Matrix"
CHAPTER 4: PERSONAL TRIALS AND TRIBULATIONS
  Love, Loss, and Grief: Keanu's Heartbreaking Losses
  Surviving Tragedy: Resilience in the Face of Adversity
CHAPTER 5: A MAN OF MANY TALENTS

Music, Motorcycles, and More: Keanu's Creative Pursuits

The Arch Motorcycle Story: Building a Legacy on Two Wheels

CHAPTER 6: THE RISE OF JOHN WICK

Reinventing the Action Genre: The "John Wick" Phenomenon

The Man Behind the Assassin: Keanu's Dedication to the Role

CHAPTER 7: KEANU, THE PRIVATE STAR

Living Under the Radar: Keanu's Quiet Lifestyle

The Man with a Big Heart: Acts of Kindness and Charity

CHAPTER 8: REFLECTIONS ON SERENITY

Embracing Zen: Keanu's Philosophical Approach to Life

Finding Peace in Chaos: Coping with Fame and Pressure

CHAPTER 9: A LASTING LEGACY

From Action Hero to Cultural Icon: Keanu's Enduring Appeal

Inspiring Generations: How Keanu Changed Hollywood
CONCLUSION
The Ever-Evolving Journey

INTRODUCTION

The Enigma of Keanu Reeves

Keanu Reeves is a personification of the complexity of contemporary celebrity, all the while keeping a distinct air of mystery that draws viewers in. His reputation goes beyond the cinema, where he is frequently acknowledged as an action star or a philosophical figure, to encompass a guy whose life narrative is replete with significant obstacles in his personal life and a tremendous capacity for empathy. People are drawn to him not just as an actor but also as a person because of this mystique.

Keanu was reared in Toronto after being born in Beirut, and his early years were marked by turmoil and grief. His resilience, which would come to define his character, was ingrained in him by his mother's tribulations in the entertainment industry and his father's abandonment. He had several difficulties from an early age, such as learning impairments and a turbulent home situation. His performances are infused with a sense of sensitivity that was fostered by these experiences. Keanu is able to engage people on a more profound emotional level because his characters frequently convey a nuanced grasp of pain and redemption.

In addition to his acting prowess, Keanu stands out in the entertainment industry for his sincere modesty and friendliness. He is known for being among the most grounded celebrities, frequently shunning the perks of being well-known. There are many tales about his generosity, whether it be in the form of charitable contributions or small deeds like offering up his subway seat to strangers or interacting cordially with admirers. This genuineness strikes a chord in a field that is often chastised for its shallowness.

Tragic events also abound throughout Keanu's life. His perspective on the world and his comprehension of sadness were profoundly influenced by the passing of his close friend River Phoenix, as well as the tragic loss of his spouse and daughter. Keanu turned his suffering into a strength instead of letting these things destroy him. He encourages people to confront their challenges and find hope in the midst of sadness by talking candidly about loss. His readiness to accept vulnerability has turned him into a resilient role model for a lot of people.

Upon examining Keanu's career, we witness an actor who embraces self-reinvention. He has moved with ease and competence across a variety of genres, from his humorous origins in the *Bill & Ted* franchise to his ground-breaking performance in "The Matrix" to the gritty intensity of the "John Wick" series. His mysterious demeanor is enhanced by each part, which highlights his versatility while staying firmly grounded in a deep understanding of humanity.

Even with his notoriety, Keanu is still a private person. He chooses a simple lifestyle over one that is extravagant, and he guards his private life jealousy. This decision heightens the mystery surrounding him and leaves followers wondering about his true nature. His outlook on life, which frequently reflects Buddhist ideas, conveys a profound inner serenity, yet the complexity of his history gives him a richness that is both realistic and idealistic.

Keanu Reeves' enigma is a celebration of a guy who, in a world where superficiality is often the norm, exemplifies kindness, resilience, and honesty. His narrative serves as a reminder that it is possible to overcome hardship, accept vulnerability, and lead a purposeful, compassionate life. Keanu stands out as a true icon, a cultural figure who inspires not only via his film successes but also through the quiet grace with which he navigates life's challenges in an era where celebrity culture typically favors image over substance.

The Mystery Behind the Man

Few celebrities in the vast and frequently hectic world of Hollywood are able to exude a sense of both brilliance and mystery quite like Keanu Reeves. Throughout his more than three-decade career, he has enthralled audiences with a staggering variety of parts, each of which captures a distinct aspect of the human experience. Keanu's performances, which range from the carefree surfer in "Bill & Ted's Excellent Adventure" to the computer hacker Neo in "The Matrix" and the unrelenting assassin John Wick, are distinguished by a complexity that frequently goes beyond the intended plot. But despite his enormous popularity, the guy behind the classic roles is still a mystery that piques people's interest.

Keanu was born on September 2, 1964, in Beirut, Lebanon, into a turbulent family environment. In search of a more stable environment, his mother, an actress, relocated the family to Toronto, Canada, after his father, a geologist, departed when he was still a small child. His perspective was shaped by this early experience of dislocation and turmoil, which also gave him a strong sense of empathy and perseverance. Growing up, Keanu had to overcome many obstacles, including academic setbacks and a slew of personal tragedies that tested his resilience. His personal life and acting style were greatly impacted by the devastating loss of his partner and close friend, River Phoenix, as well as the heartbreaking death of his daughter.

Notwithstanding these difficulties, Keanu's story is one of overcoming hardship. His personal experiences enable him to portray characters who have a deep human resonance. Keanu adds a sincerity that captivates audiences, whether it's through the existential issues of Neo questioning the meaning of reality or the frail yet ferocious drive of John Wick. Few performers can connect with audiences the way he does with his performances, which convey a profound awareness of suffering, grief, and the pursuit of redemption.

However, Keanu Reeves' mystery is not solely attributed to his movie roles. He is well-known off-screen for his kindness and humility, qualities that are a far cry from the stereotypical Hollywood character. There are many tales of his generosity, such as when he chose to give up a portion of his income to make a movie succeed or when he began using public transit and genuinely, casually connecting with fans. He is a well-liked character who is nevertheless enigmatic due to his modest personality and grounded temperament. Why, in spite of his success, does he stay so grounded? Which ideologies influence his decisions in life and work?

Why Keanu's Story Matters

The life of Keanu Reeves is not only a story of fame; it's also a moving tale of grit, kindness, and the quest for genuineness in a society that's all too quick to judge others by their appearance. In a time when being famous is often associated with abundance and excess, Keanu is a welcome change of pace. His life story is especially relevant in today's world since it embodies the battle between professional success and personal tragedy.

In a time when mental health problems are more widespread than ever, Keanu's story gives healing and hope. He freely shares his experiences of loss and sadness, demonstrating that being vulnerable is a strength rather than a weakness. Others can see that it is possible to overcome adversity and come away with a stronger understanding of oneself and the world because of his courage to face his obstacles.

Furthermore, Keanu's dedication to social duty and kindness serves as evidence of the significance of compassion in the human condition. Over the years, he has contributed generously to many charitable causes, frequently in silence, to fund cancer research and children's hospitals. His actions are a reflection of his losses and his wish to ease the suffering of others. His deeds serve as an example of a mindset that prioritizes connection above celebrity, serving as a reminder that true fulfillment stems from the relationships we form and the lives we impact rather than from awards.

We will examine the intricacies of Keanu Reeves' persona, the critical events that molded his career, and the important teachings he personifies as we go deeper into his biography. Every stage of his life, from his early years in Toronto overcoming the difficulties of puberty to his quick ascent to fame in Hollywood and the tribulations that followed, tells the tale of a successful actor and a kind person navigating life's many facets.

This book seeks to shed light on the mystery surrounding Keanu Reeves and to honor the attributes that have elevated him above the status of a mere movie star to that of a cultural icon. By telling his tale, we hope to encourage readers to embrace vulnerability, find strength in their own experiences, and see the power of kindness in a chaotic and often disorienting world. Join us as we examine the many facets of this remarkable person and the reasons why Keanu Reeves' biography is important for everyone looking for authenticity and inspiration in their own lives, not just movie buffs. We see a mirror of our common humanity in his life and work, a reminder that beauty, connection, and transformation can occur even in the most difficult circumstances.

CHAPTER 1: EARLY BEGINNINGS

From Beirut to Toronto: Keanu's Roots

The start of Keanu Reeves' career was in the vibrant metropolis of Beirut, Lebanon, far from the flash and glamor of Hollywood. Born on September 2, 1964, Keanu grew up in a multicultural and multiethnic atmosphere. Samuel Nowlin Reeves Jr., his father, was a geologist who originated in Hawaii and Native American tribes; Patricia Taylor, his mother, was an English showgirl and costume designer. Combining these various experiences gave Keanu a distinct outlook on life at a young age.

Nevertheless, Keanu had a turbulent early life. His mother went to Toronto, Canada, with him and his older sister Kim when he was just three years old, following the divorce of his parents in an attempt to start over. This change was meaningful since it signaled the start of a brand-new chapter full of possibilities and difficulties. The family had financial difficulties in Toronto; they lived in several neighborhoods and frequently relied on government support. Keanu developed a strong sense of adaptation and resilience as a result of this instability.

Growing up in a foreign nation came with its own set of challenges. Keanu struggled with the language barrier and cultural contrasts, which frequently made him feel like an alien. He went to a number of schools, one of which was the Etobicoke School of the Arts, where he initially fell in love with acting. Notwithstanding the difficulties, Keanu remained committed to blending in and becoming well-known. He accepted his new surroundings, engrossing himself in the arts and turning to performance for comfort. It was a pivotal time when he started to delve into his identity and cultivate a deep love of stories.

His mother was a strong, self-reliant woman who had a significant influence on how he was raised. Patricia's experience in the arts influenced Keanu's creative endeavors, and her unwavering encouragement spurred him to pursue his goals. She taught him the value of perseverance, diligence, and kindness—values that would serve him well throughout his life—even in the face of adversity.

Keanu developed a strong interest in acting as a teenager. He developed his skills and learned the value of performing as a form of expression by taking part in school plays and neighborhood theater productions. His performances soon attracted attention, as his innate talent was noticed. His journey took a significant turn when, at the age of 15, he was cast in his first role in a theater performance of "Romeo and Juliet". He found solace in the theater, which gave him a release from the chaos of his early years and a platform for his developing creative abilities.

Despite his increasing love for performing, Keanu had several challenges while pursuing his career. Many viewed his decision to leave high school at the age of 17 and pursue acting full-time with suspicion. Keanu was determined to forge his path and had a steadfast conviction in his ability, so he didn't let that stop him. His perseverance paid off as he started getting parts in movies and television shows, beginning with a minor appearance in the Canadian series "Hangin' In". Because of this early exposure, he was able to establish contacts in the sector and acquire useful expertise.

When Keanu was chosen to play the lead in the 1989 comedy "Bill & Ted's Excellent Adventure", it was his big break. His humorous abilities were not only highlighted in this great cult film, but it also propelled him into the public consciousness. Keanu swiftly gained widespread recognition thanks to his endearing demeanor and captivating charisma, and his professional career took off.

But Keanu always retained his origins despite his growing notoriety. He remained close to his family and thought a lot about the morals that had been taught to him as a child. He became the king and sensible person he is now as a result of the lessons he gained from his mother's hardships, his experiences as an immigrant, and the feeling of community he discovered in the arts.

Keanu's early years spent in Toronto and Beirut serve as a potent reminder of the human spirit's resiliency. His transformation from a difficult upbringing into one of Hollywood's most adored actors serves as a testament to the value of tenacity, flexibility, and pursuing one's passion. Keanu Reeves is a living example of the belief that our fates are not determined by our origins but rather by how we choose to respond to hardship and how dedicated we are to our goals.

Discovering a Passion for Performance

Keanu Reeves' career in show business started in Toronto's small classrooms and community theaters rather than a glitzy theater. He was young when he moved from Beirut and experienced the thrilling and intimidating new culture. Keanu discovered a deep emotional release and a sense of community in acting as he worked through the challenges of adolescence.

He showed an early interest in the arts and a natural curiosity for the stories and individuals that gave them life. He was especially enthralled with the transformational potential of theater—the ability of an actor to take on the difficulties, pleasures, and complexity of another person. He was drawn to the Etobicoke School of the Arts by this obsession, where he found peers who shared his enthusiasm for the arts. He was a member of a thriving community that encouraged artistic freedom and self-expression here, not just a student.

Keanu immersed himself in all facets of theater while attending the Academy, from stagecraft to acting. He took part in many shows, developing his skills and earning priceless experience. His tutors developed his ability to connect profoundly with his roles by recognizing his skill and pushing him to take chances and push boundaries. Keanu flourished in this setting, realizing that performing was a calling that spoke to his core self rather than merely a pastime.

His casting in a school play of "Romeo and Juliet" was one significant event. Keanu was given the challenging role of Romeo, which required him to portray a tragic yet passionate character. He had an intense connection to the material as he performed lines of love and grief. After this event, he realized that acting gave him the opportunity to explore the whole range of human emotions. The stage became a haven where he could communicate his deepest emotions and ideas, frequently reflecting on his own experiences.

Keanu looked for possibilities outside of the classroom as he developed his skills. He started going to television and local theater auditions, and each one strengthened his resolve to become a professional actor. The thrill of getting a part stoked his enthusiasm, the surge of adrenaline from performance, and the friendship of fellow performers. Keanu was living the art form, not only consuming it.

This route came with difficulties. The harsh reality of the profession might be discouraging, and in the early days of auditions, rejection was a common occurrence. But these failures didn't stop him; on the contrary, they made him more determined. Keanu discovered how to approach acting with a combination of commitment and humility, realizing that every encounter—good or bad—helped him advance as an artist.

After dropping out of high school to focus entirely on his aspirations, Keanu's perseverance started to pay off in the late 1980s. He was cast in a number of television shows, including the Canadian series "Hangin' In". These early appearances served as stepping stones, giving him a stage on which to display his talent and get useful experience in the business. No matter how minor the part, Keanu used it as an opportunity to hone his skills and broaden his comprehension of character depiction.

Keanu adopted a unique style for his performances as his acting career progressed. He gave his all to the roles he played, frequently devoting a great deal of time to learning about the motivations and histories of his characters. His performances demonstrated this commitment, delivering an unadulterated sincerity that struck a chord with viewers. Based on his own experiences, Keanu realized that in order to establish a genuine emotional connection with his audience, he needed to incorporate genuine emotion into his work.

His big break came when "Bill & Ted's Excellent Adventure" was released in 1989. He shot to fame with the movie, and fans all around North America connected with his portrayal of the endearing slacker Ted Logan. Not only did this part emphasize his humorous skills, but it also demonstrated his ability to develop characters that audiences could identify with. Although Keanu's excitement for performing was now entwined with the rush of achievement, he maintained his composure since he realized that this was only the start of a much longer road.

He has frequently considered the importance of those early years in Toronto throughout his career. As a young artist, he encountered several obstacles that honed his endurance and adaptability—skills that would come in handy in an unpredictable industry. His quest to find a purpose, a means of fostering relationships with people and delving into the complexities of human nature, was more important than merely chasing celebrity on his path to developing a passion for performing.

Keanu Reeves' dedication to the acting profession did not waver even as he rose to prominence in Hollywood. His remarkable career, characterized not only by box office success but also by the authenticity and depth he offers to every role, was built upon the circumstances that molded his passion for performance. Keanu's early years in Toronto gave him the conviction that narrative is a potent medium that can affect change, arouse empathy, and forge relationships between people from different backgrounds and experiences. This knowledge serves as his constant compass as he moves through the ever-changing entertainment scene, serving as a reminder of all of the significant influence that art has on the human condition.

CHAPTER 2: BREAKING THROUGH – THE ROAD TO FAME

The Rise of Ted: A Comedic Icon

The role that Keanu Reeves played as Ted Logan in "Bill & Ted's Excellent Adventure" was a pivotal one for both his professional life and the comedy film industry. When it was released in 1989, the movie fused comedy, adventure, and science fiction to create a distinctive story that connected with a generation. But it was Keanu's portrayal of the endearing slacker that made Ted a household name.

Ted's persona embodied the idealized image of the carefree youth of the late 1980s. Ted successfully negotiates the difficulties of high school with the help of his best buddy, Bill S. Preston, Esq., played by Alex

Winter, who possesses a charming mix of innocence and charm. The film's funny and creative idea centers on two dimwitted pals who travel through time to collect historical personalities for their history presentation. It deftly balances the sincerity of their goal with the ridiculousness of their journey, enabling a humorous examination of ambition and friendship.

Ted was likable and accessible because of Keanu's contagious excitement for the role. He gave Ted a carefree vibe, frequently delivering lines with a charming mix of sincerity and ignorance. Some of the most memorable scenes in the movie were built up by this unusual combination of qualities. Keanu gave Ted a warmth that went beyond simple comedic relief.

The movie's examination of friendship and the ties that develop via shared experiences is one of its most notable features. There is an obvious chemistry between Keanu and Alex Winter, which gives their shenanigans a genuine sense. The story revolves around their friendship, which highlights the value of commitment and encouragement during the turbulent adolescent years. Audiences found great resonance in this relationship, seeing themselves reflected in the follies of the two friends.

Unexpectedly popular, "Bill & Ted's Excellent Adventure" won over both reviewers and audiences. The film's cult following was made possible by its singular fusion of heart, humor, and adventure. It became a cultural sensation, inspiring video games, and animated programs as well as a plethora of goods and sequels. This popularity was largely attributed to Keanu's portrayal of Ted, which made him a household name in comedy and thrust him into the limelight in Hollywood.

In a critical sense, Ted Logan's character subverted the clichés that are frequently connected to male leads in comedies. Ted was defined by his innocence and optimism rather than by typical machismo or cynicism. His innocent exuberance was a welcome change of pace from the sometimes jaded and pessimistic viewpoints shown in other movies from the time. In addition to drawing praise from younger audiences, this portrayal won over adult viewers who found Ted's charm and innocence endearing.

Ted's reputation as a comic icon was cemented when Keanu returned to the character in "Bill & Ted's Bogus Journey" (1991) after the original movie's critical and commercial success. The protagonists' journeys were extended in the sequel, which brought fresh difficulties and experiences that put their commitment and camaraderie to the test. Keanu's performance developed further, demonstrating his ability to strike a mix between humor and reflective moments. Keanu gives Ted a stronger feeling of development and maturity as the character deals with more difficult circumstances, mirroring the changes in both Ted's and his own lives.

Ted Logan's influence on culture goes beyond the motion pictures. The character came to represent pop culture in the early 1990s and was frequently referenced in movies, TV series, songs, and other media. Ted's long legacy is demonstrated by the affectionate parodies and echoes of his catchphrases and mannerisms in a variety of media. As a result, Keanu Reeves rose to fame both outside of the comedy industry and as a household celebrity.

Furthermore, Ted Logan's persona subverts stereotypes associated with brilliance and achievement. The movie makes the argument that greatness can be attained without having to live according to societal norms. The final goal of Ted and Bill's trip is self-discovery and the understanding that genuine connection and friendship are the real indicators of success. Audiences find great resonance in this message, which encourages people to embrace their uniqueness and follow their passions—no matter how unusual they may seem.

The path Keanu took to become Ted Logan is proof of the storytelling potential of comedy. The movie delves deeper into issues of ambition, camaraderie, and self-acceptance through humor. Ted Logan's ascent to fame as a comic legend emphasizes Keanu Reeves' exceptional capacity to engage viewers on a number of levels, turning what could have been a straightforward character into a representation of hope and youthful vigor.

Speeding to Stardom: "Speed" and the Action Star

Action movie culture was about to change dramatically in the early 1990s, and Keanu Reeves was about to become a major player. In addition to securing his place as a leading man, his performance in "Speed" (1994) completely changed the course of his career and made him a legitimate action star. The picture, which Jan de Bont directed, captivated both reviewers and spectators with its intriguing narrative and exciting action scenes.

"Speed" centers on Reeves as a young police officer named Jack Traven, who has to save people who are stuck on a city bus that is set to blow up if it slows down. High stakes were inherent in the premise, and the film's pacing reflected the unrelenting suspense that built up throughout its whole running length. The popularity of the movie was greatly attributed to Keanu's portrayal of Jack, which demonstrated his ability to combine action with sincere emotion. He had to portray both the fragility of a character forced into an exceptional position and the courage common to action stars.

Authenticity was a key component of Keanu Reeves' performance in "Speed." Instead of depending just on machismo or bluster, he gave Jack a human side that made sense. Audiences were captivated by the character's early anxiety and resolve, which pulled them into the story. Keanu distinguished himself from many of his peers with this nuanced portrayal; they were not satisfied with clichéd images of action heroes. Jack Traven, played by Keanu Reeves, demonstrated the complexity of heroism by exhibiting both courage and fear.

The film's well-choreographed action scenes enhanced its visceral vitality. With its fast-paced chases and gripping standoffs, "Speed" stretched the limits of what was possible in action movies. Keanu accepted the physical demands of the part and carried out several of the stunts on his own. His devotion to realism was evident in the pivotal bus chase sequences in the movie, as he skillfully maneuvered through confined spaces and made fast movements to evoke a real sense of peril. His commitment to the role not only made the movie more realistic but also made him a flexible actor who could handle the demands of action movie production.

The famous bus jump, in which the protagonists had to jump a crack on the highway, is one of the most recognizable scenes in the movie. This scene is a masterclass in tension and timing, demonstrating the filmmaking team's exceptional expertise as well as the physical demands placed on the actors. Keanu's interpretation of this crucial scene, which combined dread, drive, and urgency, perfectly encapsulated the spirit of the movie. The excitement of the jump summed up the risks, and spectators could sense Jack's anguish as he raced against time to save the passengers.

The success of the movie was also greatly influenced by the chemistry between Sandra Bullock and Keanu Reeves. Annie, portrayed by Bullock, changes from being a passenger to an important figure in the rescue operation. Viewers were able to emotionally connect in Jack and Annie's trip because of their relationship, which brought some warmth into the midst of chaos. The way Keanu used bluster and tenderness to create a convincing bond with Annie gave the story of the movie more nuance. Their interaction, which blended romance with the excitement of the action genre, became a defining feature of the movie.

"Speed" had a significant effect on both the critics and the business's perspectives. With over $350 million in global box office receipts and multiple Academy Award nominations—including two wins—the movie became a phenomenon. With this tremendous triumph, Keanu Reeves shot to the top of the Hollywood superstar ladder. As he demonstrated that he could handle serious roles as well as high-octane circumstances that required both physicality and emotional depth, he became synonymous with the action genre.

The success of the movie also had an impact on Keanu Reeves' professional path. He was offered numerous action roles after "Speed," each of which capitalized on the momentum he had gained. Action stardom was further solidified by movies like "Point Break" (1991) and "The Matrix" (1999), which demonstrated his adaptability to a variety of subgenres. Keanu had made a name for himself in the theater industry with "Speed," a movie that made people want to see him perform.

Furthermore, "Speed" left a mark on the action genre as a whole. It established a new benchmark for how exciting scenes and character-driven storytelling might coexist in action movies. The movie's popularity proved that people wanted stories with emotional resonance in addition to spectacle. This change had an impact on later movies in the genre since producers tried to imitate the formula that turned "Speed" into a huge hit.

The part of Jack Traven continued to be a pillar of Keanu Reeves' career as he made his way through Hollywood. His transformation from a young actor trying to find his way in the business to a self-assured leading man who could captivate audiences wherever in the world was perfectly captured by the character. "Speed" was more than simply a movie; it was a turning point that demonstrated Keanu's ability and tenacity and catapulted him into an area of success that not many performers get to.

Looking back, "Speed"'s legacy goes beyond its initial box office success. It launched Keanu Reeves' career, ushering in a new phase of action filmmaking and cemented his legacy in the annals of cinema. Entertaining action, poignant depth, and endearing acting came together to produce a cultural landmark that still has a strong hold on fans. Keanu's portrayal of Jack Traven is still a lasting reminder of his journey and proof of his capacity to captivate, uplift, and amuse audiences via the power of performance. When viewers think back on the movie, "Speed" reminds them of the thrilling ride it offered and the man who played the role of the movie's hero.

CHAPTER 3: THE MATRIX EFFECT

Becoming Neo: The Role of a Lifetime

With his performance as Neo in "The Matrix" (1999), Keanu Reeves was at the forefront of a dramatic movement in the late 1990s in the film industry. The Wachowskis' ground-breaking science fiction picture not only revolutionized the genre but also changed Keanu's career and made him one of the most accomplished actors in Hollywood. The transition from Reeves to Neo was more than just a professional move; it was a significant metamorphosis that would have a long-lasting effect on both the viewer and Reeves.

Neo, formerly known as Thomas Anderson, is a complicated character. He is a disillusioned hacker who longs for the truth in an illusion-filled society. Audiences are emotionally impacted by the film's premise, which explores themes of identity, reality, and control. It mirrors the existential problems that people in contemporary society face by asking spectators to consider the fundamental nature of their own lives. Because of its philosophical foundation, "The Matrix" stands different from other action movies and offers a thought-provoking cinematic experience.

Keanu's dedication to realism is evident in the length of his preparation for the part. He spent months honing his skills and immersing himself in martial arts training and philosophy. In addition to physical skill, a thorough comprehension of the character's emotional and psychological development was necessary for the famous battle sequences. Keanu's intense training included practicing kung fu and other martial arts techniques, which were essential to Neo's development as a character. His precise motions and smooth movements captured the attention of viewers all over the world during some of the most famous action scenes in movie history, which were the result of his preparation.

The film's avant-garde visual aesthetic features ground-breaking special effects like "bullet time," in which time seems to slow down. At the same time, the camera pans around the action at regular speed, which is one of its most distinctive features. This method transformed the way action scenes were filmed and became synonymous with the movie. Keanu's portrayal in these sequences was essential; he gave the story more depth by capturing the seriousness of the situation despite the breathtaking technological effects. Keanu demonstrated his versatility as an actor by balancing the dramatic and technical demands of the part with his physique and emotional resonance.

Another essential component of the movie's story is the bond between Carrie-Anne Moss's character, Neo, and her character, Trinity. As their relationship develops from early mistrust to deep cooperation and trust, it embodies themes of love and loyalty in the face of chaos. The connection between Keanu and Moss was so strong that it pulled the audience into their romance and raised the emotional bar for the movie. Their relationship turned into a symbol of resistance against a machine-dominated world, proving that interpersonal relationships can survive even the most terrible conditions.

Neo, as portrayed by Keanu, also follows an important character arc. Neo begins his journey toward self-discovery as an average person stuck in a routine job. Along the way, he gradually begins to realize his actual potential. Many viewers can relate to this shift since they, too, feel confined by social standards. Upon discovering the Matrix and his crucial role in the battle against the robots, Neo's transformation from apprehension to self-determination inspires viewers. Viewers were able to establish a personal connection with Neo thanks to Keanu's ability to portray this metamorphosis with sincerity and sensitivity.

Following its premiere, the movie garnered both critical and financial praise, earning over $463 million globally. It developed into a phenomenon that impacted popular culture in general as well as the action genre specifically.

XThe Matrix" philosophical concerns sparked conversations about reality, consciousness, and the effects of technology on human existence. Consequently, Keanu Reeves rose from being a movie star to a cultural icon, personifying the values of independence and defiance of social norms.

Keanu returned to the role of The Matrix after the film's popularity with two follow-ups, The Matrix Revolutions and The Matrix Reloaded, both of which came out in 2003. These movies delved deeper into the intricacies of the Matrix universe while pursuing the ideas introduced in the first part. Keanu's portrayal of Neo demonstrated his unwavering dedication to the role and its consequences, demonstrating a growing comprehension of it. He was able to expand Neo's journey in the sequels by facing more difficult obstacles and delving deeper into the subtleties of sacrifice and leadership.

Neo leaves a legacy that goes beyond the movies. He now serves as a timeless representation of the fight against oppression and the pursuit of freedom and the truth. Audiences connect with Keanu's portrayal of Neo on a number of levels because it offers more than just a character in a movie; rather, it offers a wider reflection on life in general. Neo's path serves as a potent reminder of the value of challenging reality and pursuing the truth in a society where technology and false information are taking on a greater and greater role.

The transition of Keanu Reeves into Neo was more than just an acting triumph; it was a profoundly transformative experience that impacted his identity as an artist. He embraced the difficulties of physicality, emotional complexity, and philosophical inquiry as he explored new facets of his art in this role. Filmmakers and viewers alike are still impacted by "The Matrix," and Keanu's performance is still regarded as a pinnacle of cinematic brilliance.

The more time has gone by, the more important Neo has become. Numerous interpretations and analyses have been inspired by the character, who continues to be a touchstone for conversations about technology, reality, and the human experience. Keanu's performance has had a lasting impact on culture, proving the ability of narrative to inspire change and thought. Keanu Reeves' transformation into Neo not only cemented his place in the action movie industry but also made him a key player in the investigation of what it means to be a true human in a world growing more intricate by the day. Neo's voyage symbolizes a search for truth, freedom, and identity—an odyssey that still has the same power to inspire people now as it did when the movie first came out.

The Cultural Impact of "The Matrix"

When "The Matrix" was released in 1999, it became an instant classic that went beyond the genre of conventional action movies and had a profound impact on filmmaking, philosophy, and popular culture. Its distinctive fusion of cutting-edge special effects, philosophical questions, and high-concept science fiction struck a deep chord with viewers and sparked conversations that spilled out of the cinema. The movie's cultural influence can be observed in many areas of society, including fashion, technology, philosophy, and filmmaking methods.

Fundamentally, "The Matrix" raises significant queries regarding perception, identity, and reality. In an increasingly technologically-dominated world, the idea of the "Matrix"—an artificial simulation that modifies human perception—has come to represent doubting the nature of reality itself. The main idea of the movie asks viewers to reflect on how much of their lives are shaped by outside factors, reiterating current worries about media overload and digital manipulation. Because of its continued relevance, "The Matrix" is still brought up, particularly when talking about virtual reality and the effects of artificial intelligence.

The movie has had a significant philosophical impact. Its ideas have been thoroughly examined by academics and philosophers, who have found similarities between it and the writings of figures such as Descartes, Baudrillard, and Plato. Discussions concerning "The Matrix" frequently bring up the cave metaphor from Plato's "Republic," which highlights the distinction between perceived reality and true reality. Neo represents the enlightened path in philosophy, progressing from ignorance to knowledge. Its philosophical complexity has further cemented the film's place as a cultural icon by inspiring a plethora of academic courses and conversations.

"The Matrix" foresaw many of the problems with technology and digital culture that we face now. The film's depiction of a dystopian future in which people are dehumanized and enslaved by robots serves as a warning about the possible repercussions of unbridled technological growth. This is a warning that is especially relevant in this day of rapidly advancing virtual reality, AI, and surveillance technologies. "The Matrix" provides a crucial lens through which to consider the ethical consequences of technology on human existence as society works through the intricacies of these breakthroughs.

The influence of "The Matrix" also had a big impact on aesthetics and fashion. The movie popularized a new look that combined noir and cyberpunk elements with slick black apparel and eyewear. In addition to influencing fashion trends, this aesthetic evolved to represent a larger cultural movement toward a more futuristic and digital mentality. Characters like Neo and Trinity have become icons in pop culture, spawning endless homages in fashion shows, music videos, and ads. The enduring effect of "The Matrix" on modern visual culture is seen in the frequent references made by designers and artists in their creations.

Moreover, the action genre was transformed by the movie's avant-garde visual effects. Methods such as "bullet time," in which the camera pans around a still image, demonstrated a fresh approach to holding viewers' attention. This invention raised the bar for action scenes and encouraged other directors to experiment with related methods. A lot of movies after "The Matrix" tried to replicate the same energy and visual storytelling, and this is evident in those movies. It has had a significant influence on the technical side of filmmaking, resulting in CGI developments and useful effects that continue to influence the field.

Additionally, "The Matrix" created a devoted following that interacts with the movie's themes and mythology. This group has explored the complexities of the Matrix universe through the creation of fan theories, artwork, and even scholarly papers. The fans' involvement with the film was further enhanced by its sequels and expanded universe, which included animated shorts and video games. Together, these media created a complex tapestry of storylines that extended the original film's examination of reality and choice. The enthusiasm among "The Matrix" fans underscores a shared aspiration to analyze and comprehend the movie's intricate concepts, emphasizing its significance as a cultural phenomenon.

"The Matrix" has continued to influence upcoming generations of filmmakers and storytellers in the years after its debut. Its impact can be seen in a variety of mediums, such as literature, video games, and even advertisements. The film's examination of parallel universes and the nature of life finds resonance in modern storytelling, with authors attempting to imitate its avant-garde approach to character development and narrative structure. "The Matrix's" lasting influence guarantees that it will always be pertinent in conversations concerning creativity, technology, and the human condition.

When we consider "The Matrix's" cultural influence, it becomes evident that the movie is much more than just an action movie milestone. Rather, it offers a profound commentary on how society views reality, technology, and identity. Its ideas are still relevant today as we navigate a world growing more complicated and serve as a helpful reminder of the value of challenging the systems that mold our existence. By achieving this, "The Matrix" has solidified its status in the annals of film history and impacted not just how movies are made but also how we view the world around us. "The Matrix" left a lasting effect by encouraging viewers to question their preconceptions and look for the truth in an illusion-filled environment.

CHAPTER 4: PERSONAL TRIALS AND TRIBULATIONS

Love, Loss, and Grief: Keanu's Heartbreaking Losses

In addition to his impressive career accomplishments, Keanu Reeves' life has been profoundly impacted by personal tragedies that have affected his character and attitude toward life. A recurrent motif throughout Keanu's path is the interaction of love, loss, and grief, which shapes not only who he is as a person but also how he interacts with the world.

When Keanu's ex-girlfriend Jennifer Syme passed very tragically in 1999, it was one of the biggest tragedies of his life. Their relationship had been powerful and profoundly significant, marked by a strong emotional bond and a mutual love of art. Nonetheless, the couple encountered significant difficulties following the tragic death of their stillborn child, Ava. Keanu and Jennifer were both deeply impacted by this tragic incident, which left a lasting impression on them.

The couple found it difficult to deal with the ensuing anguish. Such a loss can have a heavy emotional toll, frequently resulting in feelings of regret, hopelessness, and perplexity. This loss was especially painful for Keanu because he had imagined a future with Jennifer that would be full of love and friendship. Their shared sadness took a toll on their relationship, which finally caused them to split up. Keanu's love for Jennifer was clear even after their breakup, and he still felt a great deal of her absence.

Another tragedy occurred in April 2001 when Jennifer was killed in a vehicle accident. The pain that Keanu was already experiencing was exacerbated by the loss of someone he had loved so much. His grasp of loss and the transient aspect of life was further enhanced by the shock of her unexpected death, which left him distraught. Keanu learned the value of cherishing each moment and the frailty of life from this experience of losing someone so dear. His worldview has been affected by the pain he went through at this time, which has informed his predisposition to enjoy the little things in life and his approach to others with empathy.

Keanu experienced further losses in the years that followed, which made his emotional fortitude even more difficult to handle. Kim, his cherished sister, battled illness bravely for years before losing her life. Keanu and Kim shared a strong friendship characterized by unwavering love and support for one another. As children, they supported one another through difficult times and developed a close bond that lasted until adulthood. Keanu was deeply saddened by Kim's illness and eventual death, lamenting not just her departure but also the dreams and experiences they had shared.

These bereavement experiences have had a significant impact on Keanu's personality. They have given him the humility and compassion that he carries into his relationships with other people. Keanu uses his sorrow to further his understanding of others rather than let it overtake him. He has earned a reputation for being nice and kind, frequently interacting meaningfully with his followers and lending his support to worthy causes. Because of his own experiences with loss, he is able to relate to people on a level that many find refreshing in a field that is frequently characterized by superficiality.

Keanu's public image portrays a man who has experienced a great deal of heartbreak yet still finds happiness in life. He frequently discusses the value of human connection and love, highlighting the need to help one another through difficult circumstances. Many have found solace in his viewpoint, which shows that even in the most difficult circumstances, one can overcome one's sorrows and come out on the other side with a fresh perspective on life and its transient beauty.

Apart from his charitable work, Keanu has embraced his artistic endeavors as a way to cope with his loss. His cinematic endeavors have facilitated his exploration of intricate topics pertaining to love, grief, and redemption, striking a chord with viewers who have undergone analogous hardships. His portrayals have a deep emotional resonance since they frequently display an emotional depth that stems from his personal experiences.

In addition, Keanu has shared candidly about his experience with grief, offering insight into his coping mechanisms. He has discussed the value of asking for help and permitting oneself to experience all of the pain associated with loss. This openness serves as a reminder that vulnerability is a shared human experience rather than a sign of weakness.

Surviving Tragedy: Resilience in the Face of Adversity

The life story of Keanu Reeves is a powerful example of perseverance intertwined with themes of loss, tragedy, and the strength of the human spirit. The guy behind the film embodies a story of overcoming adversity that speaks to the essence of the human experience, even if many only know him as a Hollywood star. His story is not just one of professional achievement in the film business but also a gripping account of perseverance in the face of incredibly difficult obstacles.

Keanu had a turbulent life from the beginning. After his parents separated when he was a small child, he relocated to Toronto. He had to overcome many obstacles as a child growing up in a home with only one parent, including unstable finances and many moves. In spite of these difficulties in his early years, Keanu gained a strong sense of independence and adaptability—qualities that would benefit him greatly in the long run.

Keanu's first acting endeavors gave him direction and a feeling of purpose. But just as he was starting to establish himself in the field, a slew of personal setbacks tested his fortitude. He was first plunged into the deepest depths of sadness by the passing of his partner, Jennifer Syme, and their daughter, Ava. Many would have crumbled under such severe grief at such a young age, but Keanu faced his suffering with an unwavering will. Instead of letting tragedy overtake him, he retreated inward and used his sorrow to fuel his creative and personal development.

His sister Kim, who fought leukemia for several years, passed away, making this tenacity even more evident. Her illness had a huge emotional impact on him, and they shared a link of profound love and support. Keanu's strength was demonstrated by his steadfast support of Kim during her battle and his dedication to his family. He continued to find ways to pay tribute to her even after she passed away, contributing time and money to cancer research and providing assistance to people impacted by the illness. His charitable activities show not only a desire to give back but also a profound awareness of life's frailty and the value of cherishing the people we care about.

Keanu has stuck to his belief that life should be celebrated despite its inevitable suffering despite these catastrophes. He often emphasizes the value of living in the moment and finding beauty in the ordinary. His approach to life and acting has been molded by this viewpoint, which has an impact on the roles he selects and the way he engages with others. Keanu has said that suffering teaches us empathy and compassion, and he applies these teachings to his day-to-day activities.

In the entertainment industry, where stardom can sometimes bring loneliness, Keanu has built a solid reputation for kindness and modesty. His relationships with both fans and fellow performers demonstrate a profound comprehension of human connection. There are many tales of his kindness, such as when he gave up his metro seat or surprised the team with thoughtful gifts. His own experiences with adversity have created a true appreciation for others' struggles, which is the source of these acts of generosity.

Furthermore, Keanu's perseverance is evident in his work. He frequently selects parts that speak to themes of human predicament, redemption, and tenacity. His journey of overcoming challenges is mirrored in movies like "The Matrix", where his character Neo epitomizes the struggle against injustice. His awareness of loss and resiliency gives him the capacity to give his characters depth and sincerity, which enables him to engage audiences deeply.

Keanu's resilience includes both his capacity to overcome adversity and his ability to persevere through it. He has demonstrated an incredible ability to reinvent himself and carry on pursuing his ambitions in the wake of personal disasters. This revival is demonstrated by his reappearance in the spotlight with the "John Wick" series. There is a strong synergy between Keanu and the part the man he plays struggles with loss and seeks forgiveness, which is a reflection of Keanu's personal experiences.

Beyond the big screen, Keanu's tenacity has elevated him to the status of mental health advocate. He has been candid in discussing the value of getting support and creating constructive outlets for sadness. By being open about these matters, he helps dispel the stigma associated with mental health and empowers people to face their difficulties. His advocacy is a logical outgrowth of his personal experiences, serving as further evidence that hope and healing can be found even in the most difficult circumstances.

Beyond his own story, Keanu's perseverance has an impact that motivates others to face their challenges. Many take comfort from his narrative, realizing that there is hope even in the face of extreme loss. His tenacity acts as a ray of hope, demonstrating that the human spirit is resilient and capable of thriving in the face of adversity.

CHAPTER 5: A MAN OF MANY TALENTS

Music, Motorcycles, and More: Keanu's Creative Pursuits

Outside of the movie industry, Keanu Reeves has developed a complex existence full of artistic endeavors that satisfy his wide range of passions and interests. Although he is best known for his acting career, he also has artistic interests in music, motorcycles, and other fields that highlight his passion for creation and exploration. These interests offer insight into his personality as well as how he manages life outside of the spotlight of Hollywood.

There's no denying Keanu's love of music, which has been important in forming his persona. Prior to being well-known as an actor, Keanu was a part of the early

1990s band Dogstar. Keanu was the bassist for Dogstar, a rock group that combined aspects of grunge and alternative music. Even though the band never achieved mainstream success, they were well-known in the indie music community and had a devoted fan base after playing a number of locations.

Being a part of Dogstar gave Keanu a creative outlet that was distinct from performing. He found that music gave him a way to communicate his emotions and work with others, reflecting the friendship he encountered in the film industry. Keanu's passion and energy were evident in the band's performances, proving that his creative interests extended beyond the screen. Even after the band finally broke up, Keanu's passion for music continues to play a big role in his life.

Following Dogstar, Keanu kept interacting with music in different ways. He has a history of going to concerts, helping up-and-coming musicians, and even working with them on projects that appeal to his sense of music. His enthusiasm for music is more than just a pastime; it betrays a deeper comprehension of the power of the medium to elicit strong feelings and foster interpersonal connections. His acting career has benefited from his enjoyment of music, which has given him the ability to infuse his performances with a distinct rhythm and vigor.

Another important component of Keanu's artistic endeavors is motorcycling, which stands for adventure, freedom, and a sense of connectedness to the outside world. His childhood years saw the development of his enthusiasm for motorcycles, which has since grown into a lifetime interest. Keanu has frequently talked about how the rush of riding allows him to disconnect from the demands of his celebrity and reconnect with the natural world. For him, the motorcycle symbolizes a feeling of freedom and self-discovery rather than only being a means of transportation.

He was a co-founder of Arch Motorcycle in 2015, a business that creates high-performance motorcycles that combine engineering and art. As he works with skilled engineers and designers to produce machines that are both useful and aesthetically beautiful, Keanu's endeavor is an expression of his passion for the art. Keanu's vision is reflected in the motorcycles that Arch produces; their modern styling and state-of-the-art technologies distinguish them. The motorcycling world has taken notice of the company, and Keanu's engagement has encouraged many to recognize the artistic merits of motorcycle engineering.

Riding a motorcycle is an engaging experience that helps Keanu establish a connection with the world and with himself. He frequently talks about how riding has a meditative quality to it—the freedom of the open road, the rumble of the engine, and the sensation of the wind against his skin. His enthusiasm offers him a way out of the pressures of the celebrity lifestyle, bringing him comfort and clarity. He thinks back on his experiences, reestablishes his sense of self, and obtains perspective on life via these rides.

Beyond music and motorbikes, Keanu's artistic endeavors span a variety of interests that demonstrate his flexibility as an artist. He frequently draws inspiration from a variety of artistic mediums and has demonstrated a profound affinity for literature and the visual arts. His passion for reading and writing has inspired him to experiment with poetry and writing, giving him a more expressive and intimate relationship with words. His 2011 book "Ode to Happiness" is a wonderfully designed collection of poetry and visual art that reflects his artistic sensibilities and reflective temperament.

Keanu's attempt at writing shows his desire to communicate his ideas and experiences to a global audience. The book is more than just a compilation of poetry; it's a contemplation on happiness that demonstrates his faith in the efficacy of optimism and introspection. He provides readers with an insight into his philosophical way of thinking through this work, supporting the notion that inspiration and healing can come from artistic expression.

Keanu has also pursued his love of the visual arts, especially through his interest in photography. In order to chronicle his life outside of performing, he frequently uses photography to capture moments from his trips and experiences. His image as a versatile artist is further cemented by this artistic endeavor, which demonstrates his strong eye for detail and understanding of aesthetics.

A sincere desire to communicate with people and convey the complexity of the human experience is at the core of Keanu's artistic endeavors. Through writing, music, visual arts, or motorbikes, he loves creativity as a way to express his thoughts and feelings to the world. His artistic pursuits demonstrate his dedication to authenticity and emphasize the value of keeping true to oneself and pursuing one's hobbies.

Furthermore, Keanu's involvement in a variety of artistic endeavors highlights his conviction in the transformational potential of creativity. He frequently encourages people to follow their passions and emphasizes the value of self-expression and discovery. Keanu is a ray of optimism in a world where stress and hardship frequently inhibit creativity. He shows that it is possible to pursue one's passions and appreciate life to the fullest.

The Arch Motorcycle Story: Building a Legacy on Two Wheels

The history of Arch Motorcycle reflects a deep-seated love for engineering, creativity, and the wide road rather than merely being the tale of a high-performance motorcycle firm. Founded in 2015 by Keanu Reeves and Gard Hollinger, Arch Motorcycle is an example of how two friends combined their passion for motorbikes with inventive design to create a unique brand in the custom motorcycle market.

Keanu and Gard, who shared an everlasting passion for bikes, came up with the concept for Arch Motorcycle. Their friendship, which was founded on an appreciation for one another's abilities and mutual respect, offered the ideal setting for this business venture. Gard was a skilled motorcycle designer and builder who had been customizing bikes for many years. His knowledge of engineering and design played a key role in realizing the Arch concept.

Keanu, who had been riding motorcycles since he was a little boy, said he wanted to build a machine that captured his idea of the perfect motorbike experience, and that was how the business was born. The two set out to create bikes with unparalleled performance in addition to gorgeous looks. Their objective was to create motorcycles that would appeal to both collectors and riders by fusing modern technology with traditional styling.

From the beginning, Arch Motorcycle set itself apart by emphasizing fine craftsmanship and meticulous attention to detail. Since each motorcycle is made by hand in small quantities, mass-produced bikes are unable to provide the same level of individuality. Every feature of the motorcycles, from the material selection to the frame design, demonstrates the company's dedication to fine craftsmanship.

Arch's flagship model, the KRGT-1, is a perfect example of their commitment to excellence. The KRGT-1, named for Keanu Reeves, is a formidable vehicle with performance capabilities that can compete with those of expensive racing bikes. Its sleek, muscular appearance adds to its allure. It has a powerful V-twin engine, sophisticated suspension systems, and a specially designed frame. To give riders not only speed and power but also comfort and control, every part has been meticulously chosen and built.

The KRGT-1's unique design is enhanced by its attractive appearance. The motorcycle has a sleek, timeless appearance that makes it readily identifiable thanks to its characteristic form and clean lines. Its lightweight structure is a result of the utilization of premium materials like carbon fiber and aluminum, which improves performance without sacrificing durability.

Keanu's relationship with each bike is one of the things that makes Arch Motorcycle unique. In contrast to conventional manufacturing methods, Arch's custom nature permits the co-founders to have a more active role. By actively participating in the design process, Keanu makes sure that his philosophy and vision are reflected in every motorcycle. This hands-on approach fosters a sense of sincerity and connection between the creator and the creation.

When a rider buys an Arch motorbike, they are investing in a work of art that is a reflection of their passion and commitment. Every bike is customized to the rider's requirements, taking into account individual tastes for comfort, functionality, and looks. The Arch experience is distinguished by this degree of personalization, which enables each owner to have a close bond with their motorcycle.

Beyond simply creating motorcycles, Arch Motorcycle wants to foster a community of enthusiasts who are passionate about motorcycling. Keanu and Gard have stressed the value of building relationships within the motorcycle community by planning get-together rides and events. Their sense of unity is a reflection of their conviction that riding a motorcycle is about more than simply the equipment—it's about the friendships made and the memories made along the way.

The fact that Arch Motorcycle collaborates with numerous charities and organizations is another indication of its dedication to community involvement. The business takes part in activities that raise awareness and give back to the community while supporting causes near and dear to their hearts. This charitable nature highlights Keanu's personality and his ambition to have a beneficial influence outside of the motorbike business.

CHAPTER 6: THE RISE OF JOHN WICK

Reinventing the Action Genre: The "John Wick" Phenomenon

The action movie genre's cultural cornerstone, the "John Wick" franchise, has redefined what people expect from action movies. Reviving Keanu Reeves's career and raising the bar for action cinema, the series features sophisticated choreography, stylized imagery, and a story full of themes of redemption and retribution. This phenomenon can be attributed to Keanu's portrayal of the title character, the movie' imaginative vision, and the commitment of the actors and crew.

The story started in 2014 when filmmakers David Leitch and Chad Stahelski, who are both former stunt performers, elevated their skills to the fore. Using their in-depth knowledge of action choreography and martial arts, they created a movie that skillfully combined violent combat with an interesting plot. The story centers on John Wick, a retired hitman whose happy life is upended by the death of his cherished dog—a parting present from his late wife. Wick's need for vengeance is stoked by the horrible circumstances surrounding this loss, which drives him back into the underworld he had left behind.

The film's original approach to action was immediately apparent. Wick embodies finesse, agility, and precision in contrast to classic action heroes who frequently rely on overpowering weapons and raw force. In addition to highlighting the fluidity and artistry of battle, Keanu's portrayal highlights a figure who is both extremely human and lethal. A variety of martial arts disciplines, including Brazilian jiu-jitsu and judo, are used in the fight scene choreography to create a visually stunning yet realistic approach.

"John Wick" distinguishes itself from other action movies by its dedication to character growth and emotional nuance. In Wick, Keanu Reeves portrays a man who is struggling with deep pain and loss, going beyond the clichéd action hero role. Because of this sensitivity, viewers are able to relate to him on a deeper level and want him to survive. The emotional stakes are higher as Wick makes his way through a world that requires him to face both his past demons and enemies from the outside.

The franchise's ability to reimagine the action-hero archetype is what makes it so successful. Instead of exalting violence, the movies examine the fallout from Wick's choices. The story deftly intertwines themes of devotion, betrayal, and the difficult moral decisions surrounding retaliation. With every new chapter, Wick's mental state is explored in greater detail, and he is shown to be an unwilling participant in a violent world where decisions have serious consequences. Audiences connect with this complex portrayal because it offers a novel perspective on the action genre that defies conventional clichés.

The intricate world-building of the "John Wick" series is one of its most captivating features. The movies introduce audiences to a sophisticated assassin subculture regulated by a rigid code of behavior. As a haven for criminals, the Continental Hotel takes on a life of its own, capturing the nuances and laws of this murky realm. Audiences may interact with the universe in a way that feels both grounded and fanciful, thanks to the meticulous attention to detail that goes into creating an immersive experience.

Each movie adds to the mythos surrounding Wick's persona by presenting fresh enemies and allies who enhance the story. Wick's quest is made more intricate by characters like Ian McShane's Winston and Laurence Fishburne's mysterious Bowery King, who illustrate a web of relationships that go beyond simple hostility. The show goes beyond straightforward vengeance stories thanks to its nuanced storytelling, which encourages viewers to consider topics of power, devotion, and the results of personal decisions.

Another important component of the "John Wick" series' success is its choreography. Stahelski and his crew painstakingly created fight scenes that emphasize realism and fluidity, frequently fusing weapons and martial arts in a way that feels natural. The visceral impact of each scene is increased through the utilization of genuine stunts and practical effects, drawing spectators into the intensity of the action. "John Wick" stands out from other action movies that mostly rely on computer graphics and shaky camera work because of its commitment to realism.

The film's distinctive visual aesthetic adds even more to its originality. Beautiful cinematography that perfectly reflects the grace and ferocity of the action is included in every edition. Every fight becomes a carefully orchestrated ballet of violence because of the unique aesthetic that is created by the use of color, lighting, and frame. The producers' dedication to producing a visually stunning experience heightens the story's emotional impact and entices viewers to follow Wick on a number of levels.

The phenomenon of "John Wick" has had a lasting impact on popular culture. Because of its popularity, action movies with elaborate world-building and stylish choreography are becoming more and more popular. The rise of films that attempt to achieve the same combination of intense action and emotional depth is indicative of the franchise's influence.

In addition, Keanu Reeves' career has been rejuvenated by the series, positioning him as a prominent action star once more. He has gained recognition in the profession and a devoted following because of his commitment to the role, which includes intense training and stunts. Beyond just a good performance, Keanu's portrayal of John Wick demonstrates his dedication to the role and the narrative, further cementing his place as a modern cinema hero.

Apart from its remarkable cinematic accomplishments, "John Wick" has nurtured a fan base that honors the distinct attributes of the franchise. The series' cultural relevance and the bond it creates with viewers are reflected in cosplay, fan art, and gatherings devoted to it. The movies have provoked conversations about morality, violence, and the intricacies of interpersonal relationships, proving they are more than just entertaining.

There is a ton of room to explore the concepts and characters of "John Wick" as the franchise grows with spin-offs and sequels. Every new chapter adds to the legacy of the other movies, posing fresh problems and revealing fresh information to keep viewers interested. The upcoming releases aim to explore the expanding universe of assassins and the effects of Wick's deeds, delving deeper into the mythology.

The Man Behind the Assassin: Keanu's Dedication to the Role

The portrayal of John Wick by Keanu Reeves is a masterwork of commitment and sincerity, illuminating the extraordinary lengths he underwent to bring this legendary figure to life. Keanu's dedication to the part has been clear since the beginning of the "John Wick" franchise, as seen by his comprehension of the character's complexity and emotional devotion in addition to his physical metamorphosis.

Keanu underwent intensive training in a variety of martial arts, handling firearms and stunt choreography in order to get ready for the part. He spent numerous hours studying the complex fighting techniques that characterize John Wick's battle, working closely with well-known instructors. By taking a hands-on approach, the action moments appeared natural and organic instead of staged. Beyond just practicing, Keanu was committed to playing a role where the character's abilities were not just impressive but also well-grounded in knowledge and discipline.

His training program included studying practical shooting methods, Brazilian jiu-jitsu, and judo. Keanu frequently stated that he wanted to learn the fundamentals of every move rather than do acrobatics. Because of this dedication to realism, the fight scenes became a fascinating demonstration of skill and artistry that highlighted Wick's fighting style as well as the harshness of his environment.

Furthermore, Keanu's commitment to the part included the psychological elements of John Wick. He saw the character as a severely injured person whose acts are motivated by loss, sadness, and an unrelenting thirst for vengeance. In order to make Wick seem more like a man struggling with deep sadness than just a nameless assassin, Keanu tried to convey this emotional depth. This complex depiction moved audiences, and they could relate to Wick's situation because it was based on love and loss rather than just hunger for murder.

Keanu's commitment to the filming process was evident as well. An extra degree of authenticity was added to his portrayal because he executed a lot of his stunts, which is uncommon in action movies. Due to his hands-on style, he frequently suffered injuries during difficult battle scenes but persevered through the agony because he was determined to portray the character correctly. His perseverance in the face of adversity demonstrated his dedication to providing a performance that was authentic and approachable.

Keanu added a vulnerability to John Wick that went beyond his physical attributes. He depicted the essence of a man who has lost everything by delving into the character's emotional terrain. Because of this depth, viewers were welcomed to see Wick's inner problems in addition to his violent outbursts, which increased the narrative's impact. Keanu portrays Wick as a melancholy figure whose deeds are tinged with loss and pain, subverting the traditional action hero cliché.

A major influence on Keanu's performance was the collaborative atmosphere on set. He developed close bonds with the directors, choreographers, and other actors, fostering a spirit of unity that raised the emotional bar for the movie. Because of his willingness to work together, Keanu was able to exchange thoughts and ideas, which resulted in a deeper, more nuanced portrayal of John Wick. His interactions with co-stars such as Halle Berry and Ian McShane added depth to the story and woven a web of relationships that highlighted treachery, devotion, and trust.

Furthermore, Keanu's portrayal of John Wick goes beyond conventional acting; it reflects a spirit of sincerity and deference to the medium. In addition to being a killer, he wanted to come across as a man who was shaped by his decisions, his morals, and the consequences of his past. The story of the movie, which focuses on the effects of violence and the moral complexity of Wick's world, reflects this commitment.

As the series developed, Keanu's commitment changed even more. The character's journey was expanded upon with each part, forcing him to change and mature in response to the rising stakes. He was pushed to his limitations both physically and emotionally by the demands of the character, yet he accepted these obstacles and kept pushing the bounds of his performance.

It is impossible to overstate the influence Keanu's portrayal of John Wick has had on culture. A generation of action movie directors has been impacted by his dedication to genuineness and emotional depth, motivating them to give character growth and realism priority in the genre. Beyond its short-term success, "John Wick" left a lasting legacy by changing the way action heroes are portrayed by fusing real emotional depth with physical skill.

CHAPTER 7: KEANU, THE PRIVATE STAR

Living Under the Radar: Keanu's Quiet Lifestyle

In addition to his well-known cinematic roles, Keanu Reeves is well-known for leading an incredibly modest and quiet existence. He has continuously opted to live beneath the radar and shun the conventional trappings of celebrity life, even with the enormous popularity that comes with his work. His purposeful decision to lead a quiet life is a reflection of his principles and outlook on achievement, notoriety, and personal contentment.

Keanu has remained anonymous throughout his career, which is uncommon in Hollywood. He avoids the media circuit and stays away from red-carpet events and celebrity parties, in contrast to many of his peers. Rather, he frequently chooses a more subdued lifestyle that enables him to go through life as usual. His aversion to the spotlight has helped him project an authentic persona that makes him likable to both coworkers and admirers.

His grounded manner is one of the things that makes Keanu's lifestyle so distinctive. In New York City, he frequently uses the subway, public transportation, and quiet small cafés for his coffee. These ordinary moments stand in sharp contrast to the flash and glamour typically associated with movie stars. These decisions show his humility and reaffirm his conviction that staying grounded is crucial despite his famous position.

Keanu's attitude toward interpersonal relationships is another indication of his desire for seclusion. He values deep relationships more than fleeting encounters. He is renowned for fostering close relationships and frequently prioritizes quality over number in his social network. Numerous acquaintances have characterized him as devoted, giving, and very respectful. His friendships are not transactional, as is sometimes the case with celebrity friendships; instead, they are marked by true concern and support.

Even with his enormous riches, Keanu maintains a humble way of living. It is frequently stated that he has a plain fashion sense, preferring easygoing attire that prioritizes coziness over fashion. His lack of ostentation characterizes his character; he is not motivated by material goods or the need to flaunt his accomplishments. Rather, he concentrates on the interactions and events that make him happy.

This spirit of understated generosity is also evident in his charitable endeavors. Keanu likes to keep most of his charity contributions to himself, unlike many other celebrities who like to brag about them in public. He has contributed millions of dollars without asking for notoriety to assist a wide range of causes, such as cancer research and children's hospitals. His deep empathy for those going through difficult times is a result of personal events, such as the death of his sister and close friend. These experiences have inspired him to want to help others. This dedication to giving back fits in perfectly with his aim to live a modest and compassionate lifestyle.

In a field where extreme pressure and scrutiny are common, Keanu's decision to lead a tranquil life speaks everything about his character. He has developed a persona that goes against the typical perception of a Hollywood star. His values are evident in his capacity to remain normal in the face of the praise he receives. True fulfillment, as Keanu has often shown, does not come from wealth or celebrity but rather from living genuinely and maintaining an awareness of what is important in life.

Furthermore, Keanu maintains a healthy balance between his acting job and a calm personal life, never letting his commitment to his craft eclipse it. He frequently spends time doing hobbies like writing, reading, and martial arts training. One constant in his life is his love of motorbikes and the freedom of the open road. Riding gives him a chance to get away from the bustle of Hollywood, reconnect with the natural world, and spend some alone time.

Beyond his creations, Keanu also values the arts. His love of music and his collaborations with artists are testaments to his profound respect for creation in all its manifestations. His hobbies are sincere endeavors that give his life meaning and enrichment; they are not just for show.

Keanu's receptivity to new experiences is an intriguing feature of his modest existence. He has a reputation for interacting with both strangers and admirers, spending time to learn about their lives and establish a connection. These exchanges, which are frequently posted on social media, highlight his generosity and uphold his reputation as a real person. Instead of seeing fame as a barrier, he sees it as a chance to meet people from all walks of life and spread happiness.

The contrast between Keanu's notoriety and modest way of living tells an engaging story. He has chosen a humble and contemplative path in a world where many celebrities want fame and attention. His disdain for following social norms regarding what constitutes a celebrity's conduct has allowed him to carve out a special place for himself in the public mind.

The Man with a Big Heart: Acts of Kindness and Charity

In addition to his amazing resume, Keanu Reeves is widely praised for his genuine kindness and charity, which have won over admirers all over the world. His deeds of generosity and compassion reveal a profoundly nice person who utilizes his position to improve the lives of others. These actions, no matter how big or small, show the character of a man who values compassion and humanity over notoriety and wealth.

Keanu's dedication to philanthropy, which he pursues with a gentle humility that frequently goes unrecognized, is one of his most noteworthy character traits. While many celebrities want to brag about the charity work they do, Keanu likes to work behind the scenes, contributing large sums of money to different causes without looking for attention. He has contributed to cancer research, children's hospitals, and the arts, constantly directing his charitable endeavors toward causes close to his heart.

Keanu, for example, has supported groups that conduct cancer research very actively. His personal experience—he lost his beloved sister Kim to leukemia—is the foundation of this commitment. He developed a strong sense of compassion for people suffering from comparable conditions as a result of this tragedy. In an effort to enhance the quality of life for cancer patients, he has given large donations to hospitals and research foundations in the years that have passed. His gifts frequently take the form of money for programs designed to assist families in overcoming the difficulties associated with a serious disease or experimental therapy.

Keanu has been known to visit children's hospitals and interact with patients in person in addition to making financial contributions. These visits are not just publicity gimmicks; they are a sincere attempt to lift the morale of young patients whose lives are in jeopardy. These kids love having him around, and he frequently stops to hear about their experiences, joke with them, and give them a little break from their struggles. His conviction in the value of interpersonal relationships and emotional support, especially during trying times, is shown by this personal link.

Keanu's generosity also embraces his coworkers. He is renowned for creating a happy environment on set by showing love and respect to everyone, including fellow performers and crew. His readiness to share his accomplishments serves as a common example of his generosity. For example, he is renowned for giving large incentives to the stunt squad and other crew members during the *Matrix* sequel production as a way of thanking them for their efforts and contributions to the picture. This gesture of gratitude not only demonstrates his humility but also supports the notion that success requires teamwork.

During the peak of the COVID-19 pandemic in 2020, Keanu showed his dedication to kindness in a different manner. He made donations to food banks and shelters, among other organizations helping individuals impacted by the crisis. His attempts to assist during this trying period demonstrated his capacity to attend to the needs of others and showed that compassion has no boundaries.

His considerate behaviors carry over into regular conversations. When engaging with fans, Keanu has developed a reputation for being personable and sincere. Numerous stories are circulating about admirers meeting Keanu in public places, telling him about themselves and their experiences, and Keanu reacting with warmth and kindness. He frequently makes time to smile for pictures, give encouraging remarks, and have sincere chats. His views on the value of relationships and the positive effects even a modest act of kindness can have are evident in these exchanges.

Keanu has also backed a lot of educational and artistic endeavors. He has supported a number of organizations that give opportunities to aspiring artists because he recognizes the transforming impact of the arts. His dedication to fostering creativity, whether via direct funding or by supporting art education, highlights his conviction in the value of self-expression and the arts as a therapeutic medium.

Keanu's support of mental health awareness is the best way to demonstrate the depth of his compassion. He has been open about the difficulties experienced by people dealing with mental health concerns, highlighting the importance of empathy and comprehension. Keanu encourages others to seek support and assistance by de-stigmatizing mental health conversations with his ideas on the subject. His candor encourages an atmosphere in which showing weakness is viewed as a strength, which helps to propel society as a whole in the direction of acceptance and compassion.

Keanu Reeves is a shining example of kindness and humility in a field that is typically characterized by ego and rivalry. His charitable endeavors, interpersonal relationships, and advocacy work leave a compassionate legacy that goes beyond his film career. He has demonstrated that genuine success is determined by one's influence on other people's lives, not by financial gain or public recognition, but rather by acting with love and charity.

CHAPTER 8: REFLECTIONS ON SERENITY

Embracing Zen: Keanu's Philosophical Approach to Life

Keanu Reeves possesses a special combination of humility and knowledge that both colleagues and admirers highly regard. One of the main things that distinguishes him from many of his colleagues in the entertainment sector is his philosophical outlook on life. This adoption of Zen practices demonstrates a deep comprehension of life and promotes a way of living that is based on awareness, equilibrium, and reflection.

The idea of living in the present is central to Keanu's worldview. He frequently stresses how important it is to live life to the fullest and not let regrets about the past or worries about the future consume you. This viewpoint is consistent with the core teachings of Zen Buddhism, which support awareness and mindfulness. For Keanu, this is enjoying life's small joys, such as a peaceful moment, a stunning sunset, or the thrill of riding his motorcycle on a wide road. He frequently offers observations that demonstrate his dedication to relishing these moments and discovering delight in the ordinary rather than pursuing fulfillment through recognition from others.

Furthermore, Keanu has a particularly resilient and accepting approach to problems and disappointments. He is aware that there will always be successes and setbacks in life, and he gracefully accepts this duality. Rather than pushing back against challenging feelings or situations, he faces them head-on with an open heart and mind. This acceptance enables him to weather life's storms with composure and clarity rather than implying passivity. This mindset has been reaffirmed by his path, which was characterized by both personal and professional hardships. He takes advantage of these encounters as chances for introspection and personal development rather than letting them irritate him.

Keanu's relationships with other people demonstrate his fondness for Zen. He takes a sincere approach to relationships, preferring real connections to fleeting interactions. Because he puts empathy and understanding first in his interactions, this way of thinking promotes long-lasting friendships and meaningful conversations. He frequently listens carefully and completely, which is a sign of a mindful communication style. People can openly communicate their thoughts and feelings because of his ability to be present with them and provide a safe space for vulnerability.

Keanu not only exemplifies mindfulness but also the essential Zen concept of non-attachment. He understands that material goods and approval from others are temporary and do not determine one's value. He now lives a life that values relationships and experiences over material possessions as a result of this realization. Keanu is renowned for leading a frugal lifestyle and frequently forgoing the comforts that come with stardom. He dines at modest restaurants, uses the metro, and dresses, all of which demonstrate his lack of devotion to worldly possessions. This viewpoint inspires others to assess their own life and think about what really fulfills them.

Keanu's artistic endeavors are also influenced by philosophy. He takes a very serious and respectful attitude to his work, viewing every job as a chance to delve deeper into the human condition. Because of his careful technique, he is able to depict characters that are meaningful and accessible while still having emotional depth. He is aware that acting is more than just putting on a show; it's an investigation of the human condition, a concept that runs throughout his body of work. His dedication to honesty is shown in his artistic integrity, which he uses to present stories that have a deeper emotional impact.

His philosophical views are also reflected in his passion for martial arts. Keanu has received substantial training in sports like Brazilian jiu-jitsu and judo, which place a strong emphasis on focus, discipline, and respect. These exercises help him develop mental toughness and clarity in addition to improving his physical capabilities. He frequently discusses the meditative qualities of martial arts, where a deep sense of inner serenity is attained via the integration of movement and attention. This affinity for martial arts, which embodies the balance between body and mind, is a wonderful fit with his Zen-inspired way of living.

Keanu's philosophical perspective is also influenced by his curiosity about life's mysteries and his receptivity to spirituality. He is open to the unfamiliar and never stops being curious about his surroundings. This feeling of awe encourages him to pursue knowledge and comprehension throughout his life as he tries to comprehend the intricacies of life. He frequently muses on the interdependence of all creatures, stressing the value of love and compassion in navigating the human experience. This more expansive way of looking at the world encourages empathy and understanding by getting others to reflect on their role in life's larger picture.

Keanu has emerged in recent years as a representation of optimism and grit, a ray of hope in an uncertain world. Many people find inspiration in his philosophical outlook on life, which encourages them to practice mindfulness, acceptance, and compassion. He inspires others to examine their own lives and seek a path of honesty and fulfillment by living according to these ideals.

Finding Peace in Chaos: Coping with Fame and Pressure

Keanu Reeves demonstrates an amazing level of poise and reflection when navigating the challenges of celebrity. His approach to finding calm in the middle of chaos is distinctive in an industry that is frequently characterized by chaos, scrutiny, and unrelenting pressure. His capacity to handle the pressures of celebrity life says a lot about his character and inner fortitude, demonstrating how he keeps his true self in the face of enormous pressure from the outside world.

Fame can be a fickle creature, bringing with it a deluge of both favorable and unfavorable attention. Being in the spotlight can cause anxiety, nervousness, and a crippling sense of loneliness in many people. Keanu has, nevertheless, been able to approach his celebrity status from a neutral standpoint. He understands that although celebrity can lead to possibilities and open doors, it also presents a set of difficulties that must be carefully navigated.

The core of Keanu's coping strategy is his capacity to preserve a distinct sense of self. He knows that his identity and worth are not defined by the image that the general public has created of him. He can keep his personal and professional lives apart because of this separation, which acts as a buffer against the cacophony of public opinion. Keanu is able to concentrate on his work, relationships, and personal development because of his grounded temperament. He can weather the storms of fame without losing sight of his true self by cultivating this self-awareness.

Keanu's emphasis on deep connections is a crucial component of his strategy for handling stardom. He has kept his inner circle of close friends and family members small throughout his professional life. These relationships bring him a sense of security and support, enabling him to confide in people who really get him and talk about his struggles, victories, and anxieties. Keanu creates a solid support system by cultivating sincere relationships, which provide motivation and a feeling of community—two things that are crucial for preserving mental health amid the demands of being a famous person.

In addition, Keanu lives by a grateful mentality, which is a big part of why he can handle outside pressure. He frequently conveys gratitude for the chances he has been given, recognizing the assistance of his supporters, associates, and the film business. Because of his thankfulness, he is able to view barriers positively and sees them as chances for growth rather than as burdens to be overcome. He develops resilience by keeping his mind on the good things, which enables him to handle hardship with poise and assurance.

His penchant for reflection and seclusion partly influences Keanu's capacity to find calm amid upheaval. He looks for quiet times all the time, whether it be for reading, meditation, or just taking in the scenery. He gains the perspective and clarity necessary to handle the challenges in his life from these times of introspection. He can rejuvenate and reestablish a connection with his inner self through solitary activities, which enables him to maintain his composure even in the face of overwhelming external demands.

Keanu also follows the mindfulness philosophy, which helps him even more in handling his celebrity. Being totally present and nonjudgmentally involved with one's thoughts and feelings is encouraged by mindfulness. Keanu can see the commotion around him without getting sucked into it by engaging in mindfulness practices. Because of this understanding, he is able to handle difficulties with composure and clarity as opposed to hastily reacting to pressures. His commitment to practicing mindfulness is a valuable asset in helping him keep his mental stability in a turbulent world.

Keanu manages to maintain an astonishing level of composure in the face of criticism and scrutiny. He is aware that opinions held by the general public might change quickly and that what is said about him may not always be accurate. He can handle unfavorable attention with dignity thanks to this realization, and he frequently uses humor and humility to deflect unfair criticism. He concentrates on what he can control, such as his decisions, actions, and the energy he contributes to the world, rather than letting other people's opinions determine his sense of value.

His encounters with loss and hardship have also influenced Keanu's perspective on the transience of life. Having experienced personal traumas, such as the death of close ones, he has a deep appreciation for the little moments in life. His determination to live completely and honestly, unencumbered by social conventions, is strengthened by his realization of his mortality. He finds comfort in vulnerability and encourages others to face their struggles bravely and honestly by doing the same.

Reeves is a perfect example of how self-awareness, thankfulness, and mindfulness can help one find calm in the midst of celebrity mayhem. His strength and character are demonstrated by his ability to handle the demands of being a celebrity while staying true to who he is. He provides a haven of peace in the midst of chaos by cultivating deep relationships, engaging in acts of gratitude, and appreciating his alone time.

In a society where being famous may frequently result in stress and disillusionment, Keanu's path stands as an example. His way of thinking inspires people to value authenticity, pursue balance, and develop resilience. Keanu Reeves not only manages his popularity through his actions and thoughts, but he also uses it as a platform for inspiration and positivism. By doing this, he serves as a reminder that, even in the midst of chaos, focused living and a close bond with people and oneself may lead to calm.

CHAPTER 9: A LASTING LEGACY

From Action Hero to Cultural Icon: Keanu's Enduring Appeal

The transformation of Keanu Reeves from action star to cultural icon illustrates the changing nature of celebrity and the strong bonds he has built with fans all around the world. His enduring appeal is based on a special fusion of charm, humility, and a sincere love for his work, which goes beyond the usual bounds of celebrity. This change demonstrates not only how his profession has developed but also how larger societal changes have impacted his effect and identity.

Originally known for his parts in fast-paced action movies, Keanu gained popularity after a run of hits, which made him a leading Hollywood man. His physical strength and charisma on screen helped him establish himself in the action genre with roles in movies like "Point Break" and the "Matrix" trilogy. Nevertheless, his genuineness and relatability struck a deep chord with the audience, drawing them into more than just his skill at stunts and combat scenes. Keanu frequently portrayed the everyman in his roles—someone who faces overwhelming adversity yet never gives up. This bond with his characters made it possible for audiences to identify with him and his performances, which created a sense of devotion and respect that went beyond the screen.

As his acting career developed, Keanu distinguished himself from many of his peers by his dedication to his characters. He devoted himself to each character in a way that went beyond appearances. He had extensive training in martial arts and weapon handling, for instance, in order to ensure that his portrayal of "John Wick" was not only credible but also respectful of the genre. Fans of his have grown to love him even more for his meticulous attention to detail and reverence for the craft, as well as his willingness to go to great lengths and devote himself entirely to his characters. His genuineness in the face of extreme physical strain reflects his overall life philosophy, which embraces obstacles and turns them into chances for development.

The pivotal moment in Keanu's transformation from action star to cultural icon can be attributed to his handling of the difficulties that come with stardom and personal hardship. His humility and fortitude have influenced the public's opinion of him in the face of tragedy, including the death of loved ones. Rather, he represents a personification of compassion and tenacity, traits that are relevant in a culture that is more and more looking for genuineness and community. Because of his experiences, he is able to relate to audiences on a far deeper level than he could have in his on-screen personas.

The popularity of social media in recent years has been a major factor in increasing Keanu's cultural relevance. In a world of celebrities where vanity and excess are common, his interactions with fans—marked by compassion and genuine interest—have made him a symbol of positivism and humility. Moments that went viral, like his conversations on public transportation or his sincere admiration for fan art, have strengthened this impression. These insights into his private life show a man who, in stark contrast to the sometimes romanticized personalities of Hollywood stars, is personable and grounded. Because of his relatability, he has been able to go beyond the conventional bounds of celebrity and maintain his place as a popular person.

Furthermore, Keanu's casting decisions further highlight his cultural relevance. He still excels in action movies, but he has also dabbled in other genres to show off his versatility as an actor. The films "A Scanner Darkly" and "The Lake House" demonstrate his openness to delving into intricate storylines and tackling provocative subjects. This adaptability not only broadens his repertory but also reinforces his status as an actor who doesn't mind shattering stereotypes. Viewers are drawn to his adaptability and the genuineness he offers to each job, which speaks to a wider cultural appeal. He can switch between genres with ease.

The recent spike in interest in his movies, especially the "John Wick" series, demonstrates a fresh understanding of his significance to the motion picture industry. Audiences have responded well to the franchise's blend of stylized action, emotional depth, and philosophical implications, making Keanu a key player in the reshaping of the action genre. The relationship between Keanu and the character feels natural and genuine since John Wick is a man who is struggling with loss and looking for forgiveness. His professional decisions and personal convictions are in line, which increases his cultural relevance and makes it possible for audiences to interact with his work on several levels.

Beyond the big screen, Keanu's humanitarian endeavors and little deeds of kindness serve to solidify his reputation as a national treasure further. His charitable contributions, frequently given in secret, to cancer research and children's hospitals show a strong dedication to helping others without expecting praise in return. In a society where self-promotion usually takes precedence over generosity, this selflessness strikes a chord. His fans are grateful that he makes good use of his platform, adding to a story that takes him above and beyond the typical celebrity status.

Keanu Reeves is a cultural icon who personifies a complex combination of traits that are relevant in today's world. His path is a reflection of the difficulties associated with celebrity, the value of genuineness, and the strength of perseverance. He invites us to reevaluate what it means to be a hero both on and off the screen by challenging preconceived ideas about celebrity through his capacity to engage audiences on a human level.

Inspiring Generations: How Keanu Changed Hollywood

As a key figure in Hollywood, Keanu Reeves inspires generations not just with his performances but also with the ideals he upholds and the changes he has sparked in the business. Beyond the screen, his influence reflects a greater societal trend toward sincerity, modesty, and perseverance in the face of hardship. Analyzing Keanu's professional path reveals how he has revolutionized the definition of a Hollywood star, making a lasting impact on both the business and its consumer base.

Keanu's acting style was unconventional from the beginning, going against the grain of Hollywood's leading men. During a time when action movies were mostly about machismo and bravado, he gave his characters a welcome depth and sensitivity. Keanu offered a feeling of reflection and emotional complexity to his roles, whether he was playing the reluctant hero in "John Wick" or the troubled Neo in "The Matrix," which connected with audiences. This break from conventional action tropes opened the door for a new wave of actors to take on parts that value emotional realism over raw physicality. Because of Keanu's success in these parts, audiences have shown a hunger for nuance and complexity, which encourages aspiring performers to explore their emotional range rather than fit into preconceived notions.

Hollywood has also been more open to investigating original stories as a result of Keanu's persistent preference for unusual storylines. His work on "The Matrix" with visionary filmmakers like the Wachowskis opened opportunities for further creative filmmaking, fusing action, science fiction, and philosophy. This audacious strategy pushed studios to spend money on innovative material that questions the established order, thereby expanding the canon of stories in mainstream film. More varied tales that capture the complexity of the human experience have consequently come to light. The innovative narrative is now not just accepted but applauded in society thanks to Keanu's work, encouraging other filmmakers to take artistic chances.

Keanu's ideology has profoundly impacted Hollywood. In a field where extravagance and ego are common, his modesty and grounded manner have redefined the expectations for how celebrities should engage with their followers and their art. As demonstrated by his viral moments conversing with fans and expressing gratitude for their support, viewers find his genuine friendliness and approachability to be relatable. The industry's culture of humility and thankfulness has been fostered by this emphasis on honesty and respect, which has motivated both seasoned performers and up-and-coming performers to value sincere ties with their audience.

In addition, a lot of people have found encouragement in Keanu's ability to bounce back from personal sorrow. His perspective on life has been profoundly affected by the major losses he has experienced, such as the passing of his close friend River Phoenix and the stillbirth of his daughter. Instead of letting these things break him, Keanu has used his sorrow to become more aware of the beauty and fragility of life. His graceful handling of such deep grief encourages people to face their struggles head-on with bravery and resiliency. His genuineness in overcoming personal adversity has won him over both admirers and fellow performers, proving that vulnerability is a great virtue rather than a weakness.

Keanu's dedication to charitable projects emphasizes even more how amazing he is. His charitable endeavors, which are frequently carried out subtly and without much fanfare, reveal a strong sense of social duty. He has contributed to several causes, including as cancer research, children's hospitals, and charitable groups that help the less fortunate. Redefining what is expected of celebrity activism, this commitment to giving back without seeking acclaim has encouraged other stars to use their platforms for social good. Keanu promotes a philanthropic culture in Hollywood by serving as an example of how fame can be used for good, demonstrating that true popularity is about more than just one's success—it's also about bringing others up.

Keanu's standing as a cultural icon has been reinforced in recent years by the rebirth of interest in his work, especially with the success of the "John Wick" trilogy. In addition to showcasing his acting and physical prowess, the franchise emphasizes themes of violence's aftereffects, loyalty, and redemption. These stories strike a profound chord with viewers, provoking moral and individual decision-making debates. Keanu encourages viewers to consider their morals and decisions by playing a nuanced antihero, which deepens their connection with the story. A new generation of filmmakers and storytellers has been impacted by his ability to inject philosophical depth into action-packed storytelling, proving that entertainment has the power to promote change and encourage thinking.

Keanu's path also serves as a reminder that one's influence on others matters more than box office receipts or accolades when determining success. His unwavering emphasis on poignant narrative, profound emotional resonance, and sincere interpersonal relationships highlights a larger Hollywood cultural change toward the appreciation of honesty and sincerity. Keanu has thereby encouraged a more deliberate approach to filmmaking and audience involvement, motivating a new generation of actors, directors, and enthusiasts to place a higher value on storytelling that connects on a human level.

CONCLUSION

The Ever-Evolving Journey

As our investigation of Keanu Reeves comes to an end, it is evident that his life and profession have been shaped by a constantly changing path characterized by resiliency, genuineness, and a strong bond with people. Fans of all ages regard Keanu as a complex person whose experiences, both on and off screen, arouse respect and adoration. He represents an unrestricted celebrity who consistently pushes the envelope of what it means to be a successful actor and a kind person.

As we look to the future, we wonder: what will happen to Keanu Reeves? Keanu is still leading the way in the ongoing evolution of the cinema business. His more recent endeavors, such as the "John Wick" series, have cemented his status as an action star and demonstrated his aptitude for handling intricate storylines that appeal to contemporary audiences. Fans are interested in seeing how he will continue to reinvent himself as he takes on new roles and endeavors. Keanu's commitment to his work implies that he won't hesitate to take on difficult roles that foster both creative and personal development. In a world where people are looking for depth and significance, his involvement in initiatives that explore themes of morality, redemption, and the human experience will have an even greater impact.

Furthermore, Keanu's enthusiasm for telling stories and his readiness to work with creative directors portend a bright future. His dedication to pushing the envelope in the movie industry raises the possibility that he will experiment with new forms or genres, possibly taking on roles that combine intensely emotional storytelling with action. Given the renewed interest in interactive storytelling and virtual reality, Keanu might be seen as a trailblazer in these new media. His innovative vision, along with the boundless possibilities of technology, could result in ground-breaking experiences that interact with viewers in fresh and significant ways.

A few themes that go beyond entertainment come to light when we consider the lessons to be learned from Keanu's life. His story is a powerful example of resiliency in action. Keanu has shown a persistent character that encourages others to persevere in their own life, even in the face of significant personal hardships and losses. He reminds us that strength is measured not just by accomplishment but also by the bravery to face one's anxieties and problems head-on. This is demonstrated by his ability to embrace vulnerability while navigating the complications of celebrity.

Moreover, Keanu's modesty imparts a valuable lesson on genuineness. In a time when celebrity culture frequently encourages self-promotion and superficiality, Keanu's grounded demeanor serves as a reminder of the value of staying true to oneself. His generosity to others, whether in the form of charitable endeavors or small tokens of appreciation, shows a profound awareness of the interdependence of all people. This focus on compassion highlights the value of kindness in a society where people can occasionally feel alone and inspires them to cultivate real connections in their own lives.

Keanu's journey also highlights the importance of ongoing development and reinvention. He has welcomed change throughout his career, rising to the occasion and developing as a person and an actor. Others are motivated to approach their travels with an open mind and heart by this eagerness to learn and develop. Accepting new experiences in one's personal or professional life can serve as a potent reminder that change is a constant on this trip and that everyone is capable of it.

Keanu Reeves's dynamic journey serves as a tribute to the strength of human spirit, resiliency, and genuineness. His work, principles, and actions continue to inspire audiences worldwide, demonstrating his limitless potential as a star. His narrative serves as a reminder that a cultural icon's genuine essence is found in their ability to positively influence others' lives in addition to their level of recognition. We know that Keanu's journey will continue to inspire us all to embrace our pathways with bravery, generosity, and an unrelenting commitment to authenticity as he navigates the next chapters of his life and career. Generations to come will surely find inspiration in the principles he taught us, inspiring us to live lives full of meaning, kindness, and adventure.

www.ingramcontent.com/pod-product-compliance
Lightning Source LLC
Chambersburg PA
CBHW050309230526
45471CB00005B/2101